IF DOGS COULD SWEAR

IF DOGS COULD SWEAR

Adrian Searle
& Judith Hastie

Published in the UK October 2013
Freight Books
49-53 Virginia Street
Glasgow, G1 1TS
www.freightbooks.co.uk

A CIP catalogue reference for this book is available from the British Library

ISBN 978-1-908754-26-4
eISBN 978-1-908754-27-1

Printed and bound by Bell and Bain, Glasgow

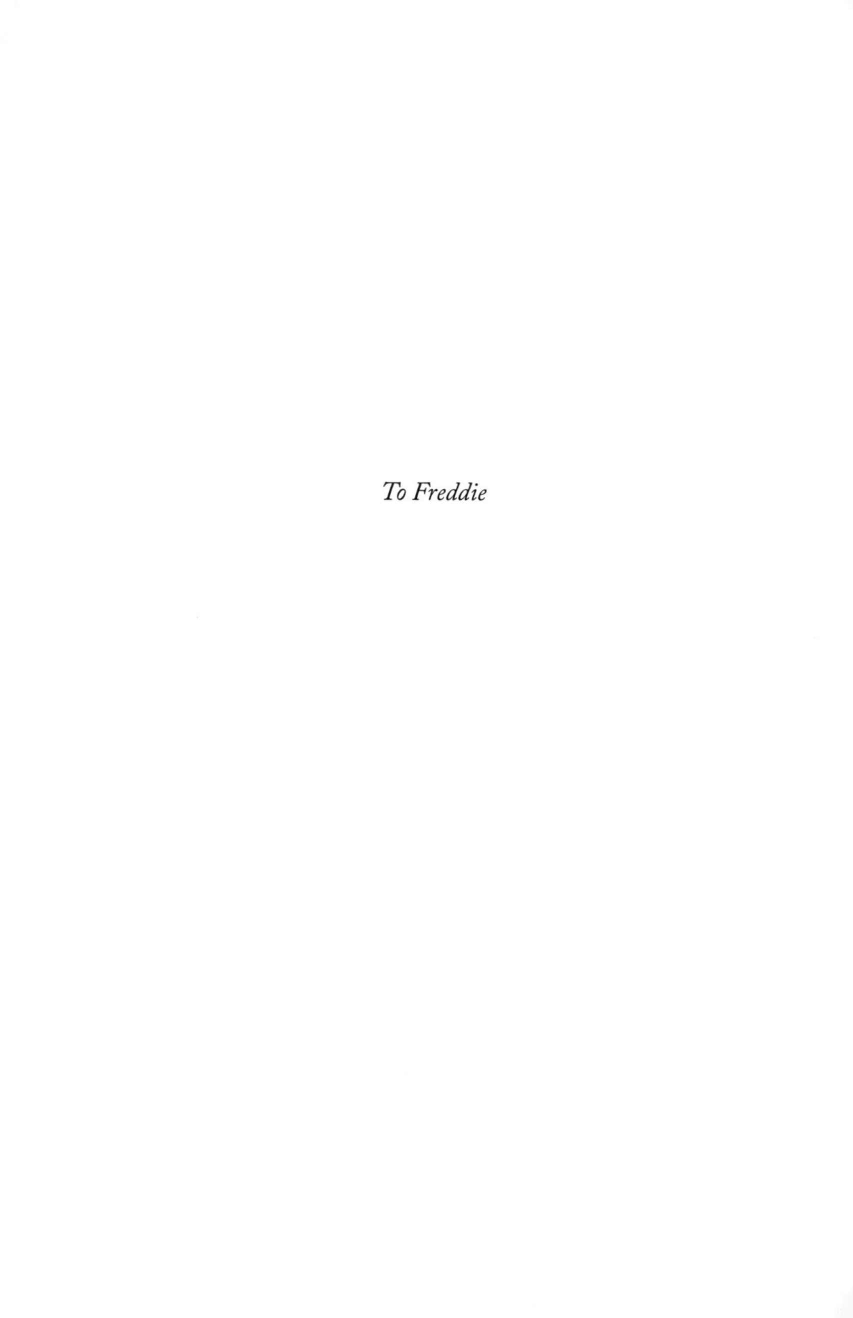

To Freddie

Introduction

A dog is a woman's and a man's best friend, so the ancient dictum goes. But do you ever look at your beloved canines and wonder just what's going on in their furry little heads? We like to think that dogs are benign, selfless and devoted. But what if they aren't? What if they're really like us?

As the proud owner of a Bichon Frise, and former owner of a Jack Russell, there have been moments where I've thought I've caught a look of contempt, cynicism or just plain irritation on my pet's face, usually because of something I've done that defies comprehension in the dog world. And I can't help but suspect that often our dogs are tolerating us much more than we ever tolerate them.

With this in mind, Judith Hastie and I embarked on *If Dogs Could Swear*. I hope that many of the scenarios included are instantly recognisable. Certainly, many of them are inspired by my own personal experiences as a dog owner.

This book isn't for the faint-hearted or the easily offended. But at the heart of every pooch, I believe, is a pragmatism and lack of squeamishness that puts us to shame. Read on and enjoy – and you never know – at the end of this book, you might just understand your dog a little bit better.

My arse isn't itchy, it's just the static from this carpet makes my balls tingle

And while you're there, could you dislodge that Rolex I swallowed?

Say hello to my little friend

If we see that sexy bitch from No 43
you're on your fucking own, mate

So glad you're home... I shat all over the dining-room and now I need you to clean it up

This little gizmo helps me smell out rotting roadkill with 45% improved accuracy

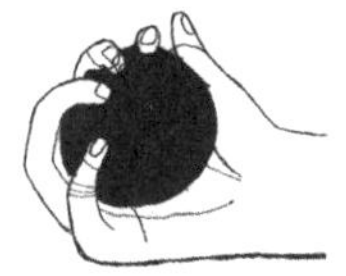

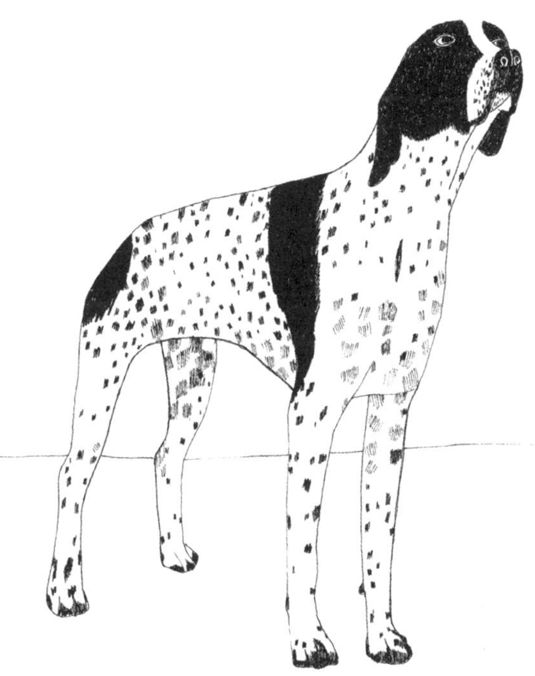

If you do that pretend throw thing again,
I'm going to sink my teeth into your fucking crotch

I'm getting gooseberries, cabbage and clams, with notes of horsemeat

And since it's my birthday, I suppose a butt plug is out of the question?

You may have just given me this, but you're still a twat

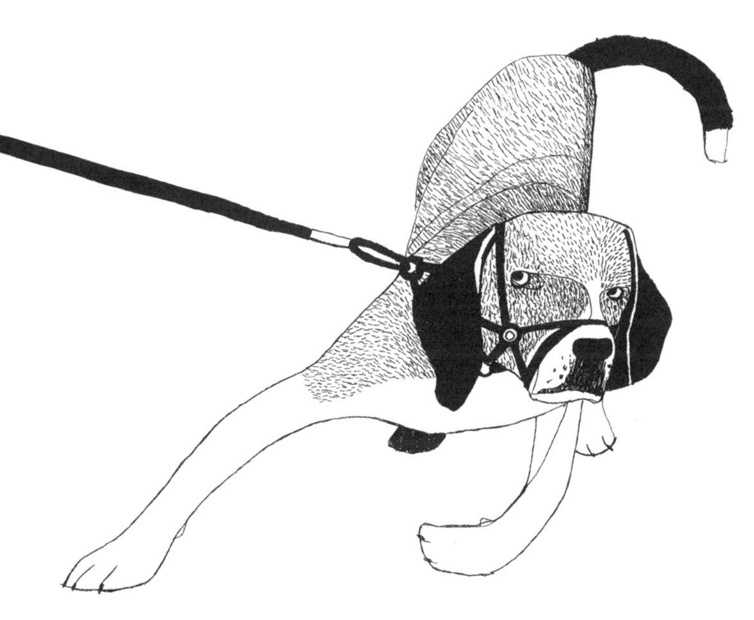

I like a bit of bondage as much as the next dog but you guys are fucking obsessed

You stick me in this stupid fucking hat,
I leave you little present under tree

Hey, this shit really keeps!

I don't enjoy this you know, I just don't trust the motherfucker who's driving

One more generation of in-breeding and we might manage to create a dog that really does have two dicks

You've just left me in fucking kennels for two weeks. All I can say is, from now on, put on your shoes with care, my friend.

Serves you right for buying that piece of shit from DFS

And I had to be bought by a gay couple…

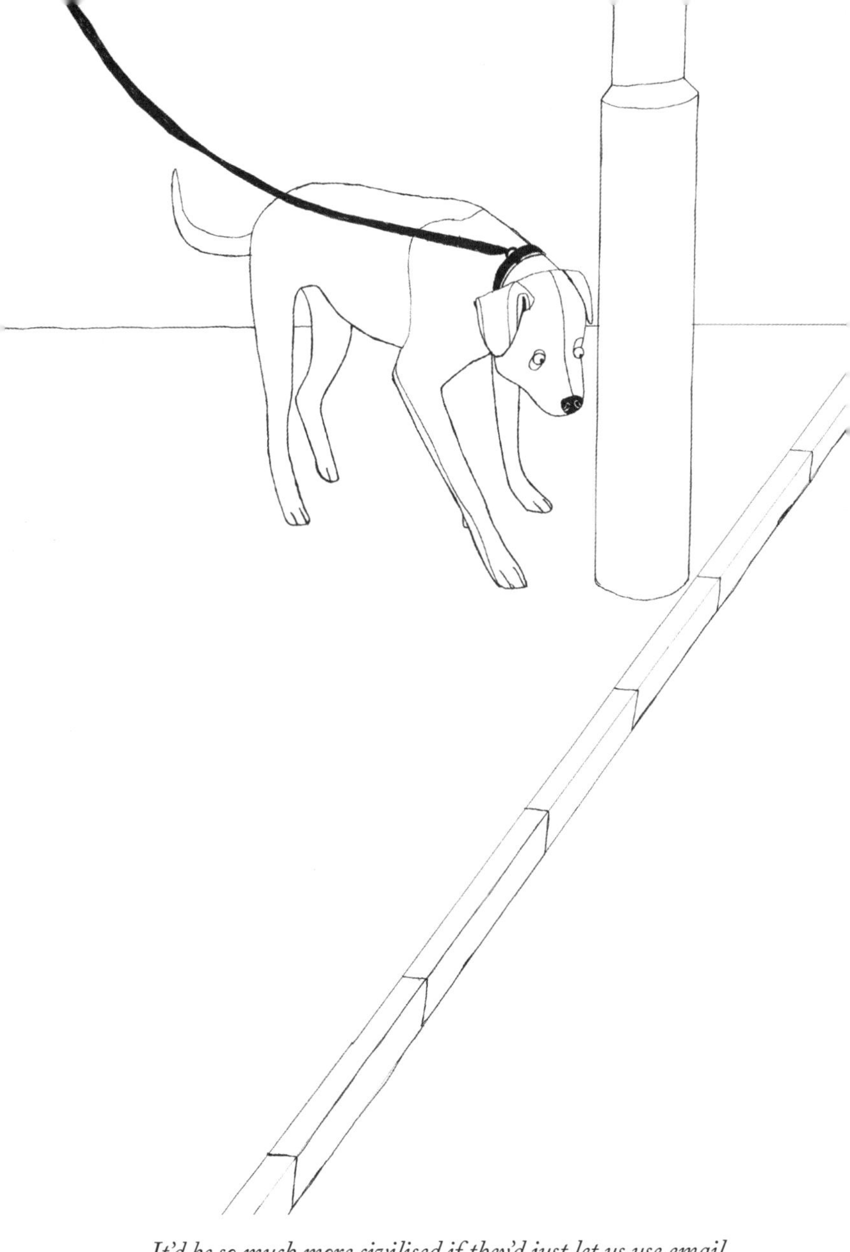

It'd be so much more civilised if they'd just let us use email

It may be fox poo to you, but its Chanel No 5 to me

I've finally finished my novel – it's called 50 Shades of Brown

Ha! They picked me, you bunch of in-bred fuckers!

Yeah, I'm with fuckface up there

It's so bloody cold my balls could drop off,
if you bastards hadn't cut them off already

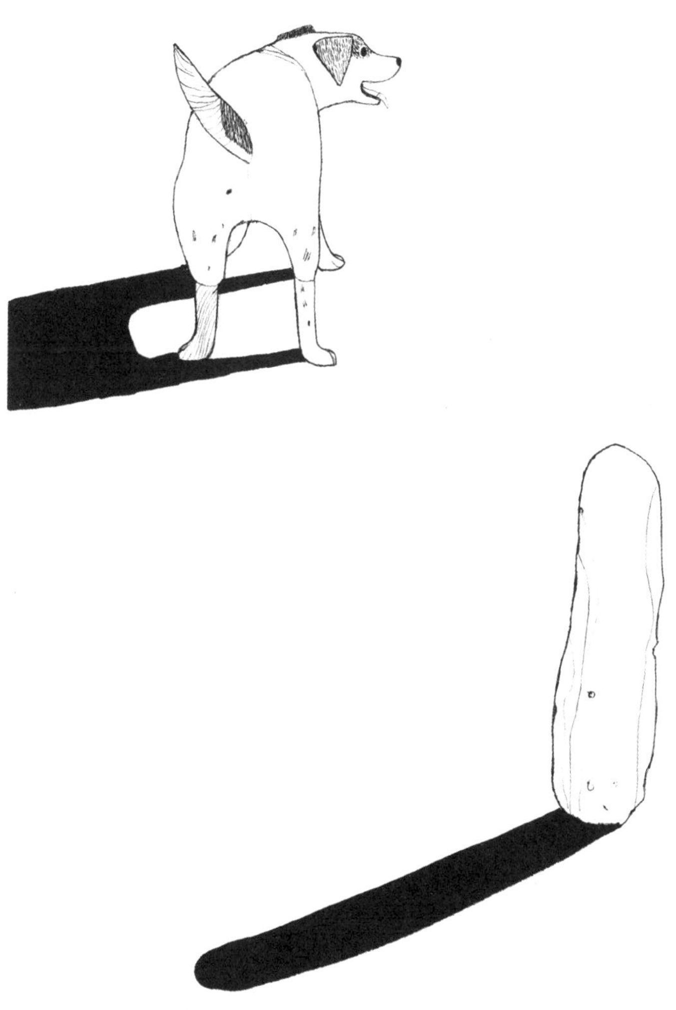

65 dog years and I've finally managed to shit one on its end!

I've got fifty friends on faecesbook

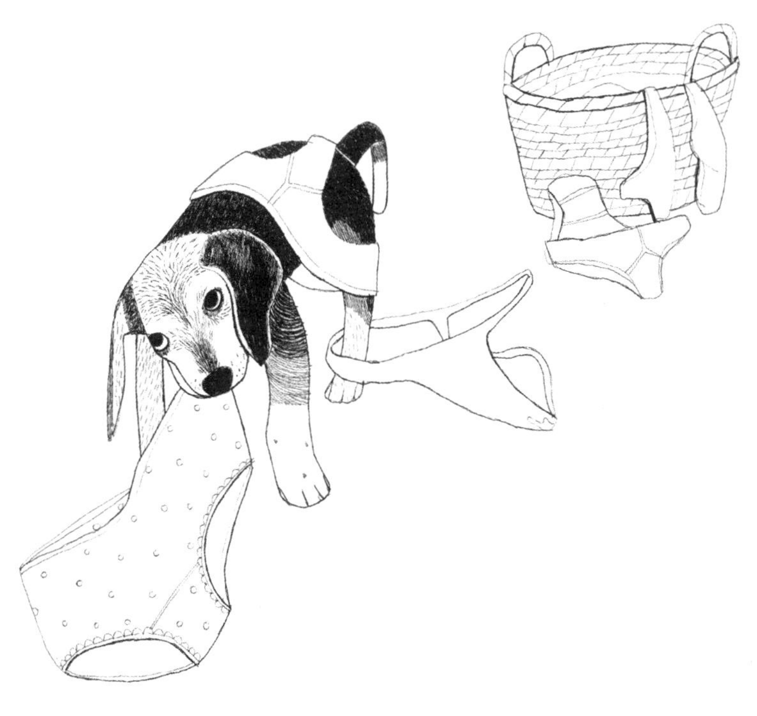

It's the ones that have been marinating in the linen basket for a week I love the most

You won't think I'm so cute when I give you fucking rabies

Maybe if the dickhead thinks I'm dead he'll leave me alone

You're gonna have to be bloody fast if you're going to catch me before I vomit on your new carpet

No offence, but I'd rather be seen by another dog, if you don't mind

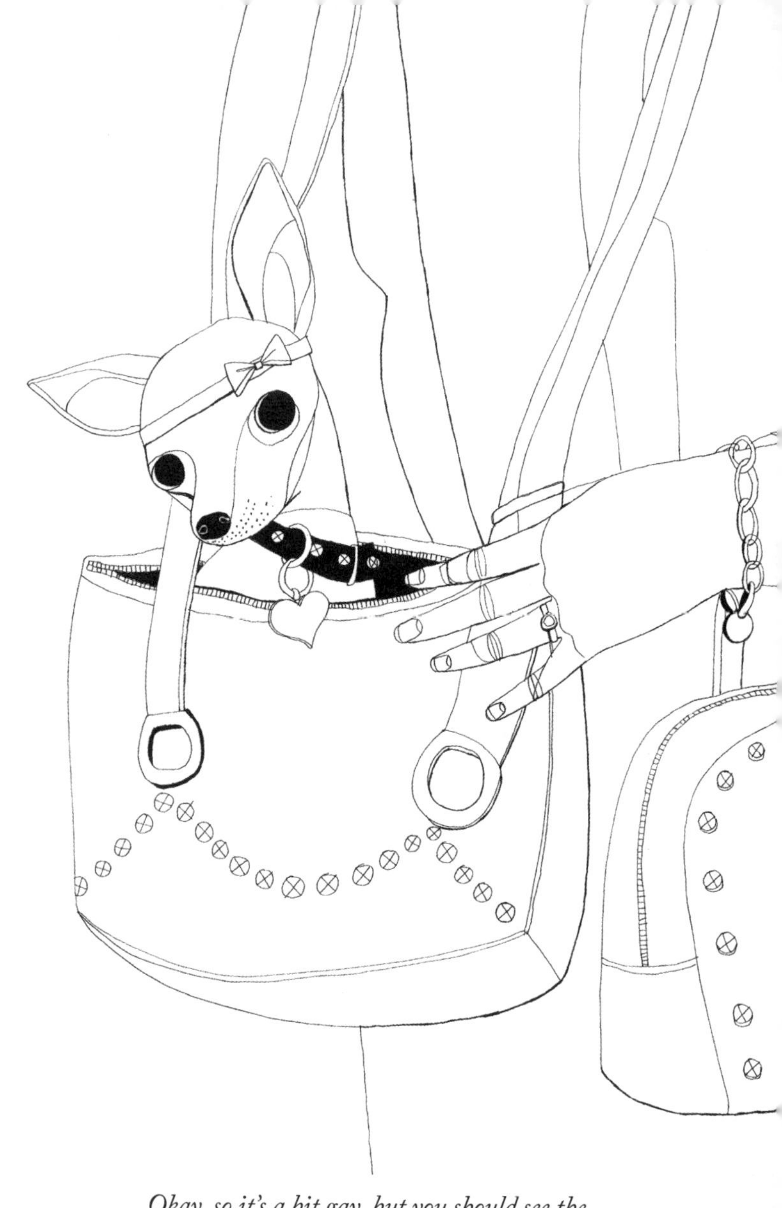

Okay, so it's a bit gay, but you should see the prescription drugs the bitch has got in here

It's not enough to cut my knackers off,
you've got to do this to me as well

Not only does this kerchief make me look like a twat, that waistcoat you're wearing confirms you really are a lesbian

Seriously impressive boner, mate

I find that Inland Revenue tax rebates taste the best

She thinks I'm doing this because dogs like to chew,
but I'm actually doing it because I hate the cow

You know what they say… small dog, huge shit

I love the smell of old piss in the morning...

You bastards can't prove anything

You can kiss my furry arse if you think I'm going out in that

Yes, my name is Hannibal. And, yes, I am a fucking cannibal.

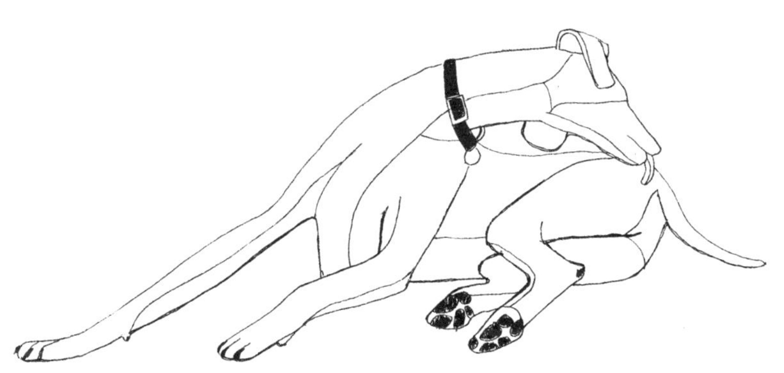

Ok… I admit it, I'm a crack addict

The irony is, I can't hear a fucking thing

Lassie never had to wear one of these fucking things

It's the all pervading smell of shit that gets me horny

I haven't time for this rescue shit, I've an AA meeting in 15 minutes

The haircut is bad enough but why do you have to go in for this kinky BDSM bollocks?

Seriously, I've got to be in a kennel with a dick like you?

Okay, so it's not exactly true love, but when you gotta crack one off…

Why is it always bad dog? Why not bad cat… or bad hamster?

You want me to want this treat don't you?
Well, I'm just faking it… like that girlfriend of yours.

Greetings, I am the fabled dog with two dicks, and yes, I AM fucking pleased

My therapist told me that I'll feel better about myself if I perpetrate a bit more wanton destruction each day

I know I'm your best friend, but stop bloody staring, you're creeping me out

If I keep working at it, one day my bite WILL be worse than my bark

I drag you out of a burning building – and you do this to me?

We're not the only pair of new puppies she's got

What a hypocrite. He makes me carry this shit in my mouth but won't let me eat poo off the ground.

Who doesn't like fucking bath time now?

According to this nose of mine, she's ovulating.
I'd get the fuck out of here if I was you, mate.

Okay, I know I got excited and showed her my crayon,
but just remember, I'M your best friend.

Get up and make my breakfast, you lazy bastards. It's 6am.

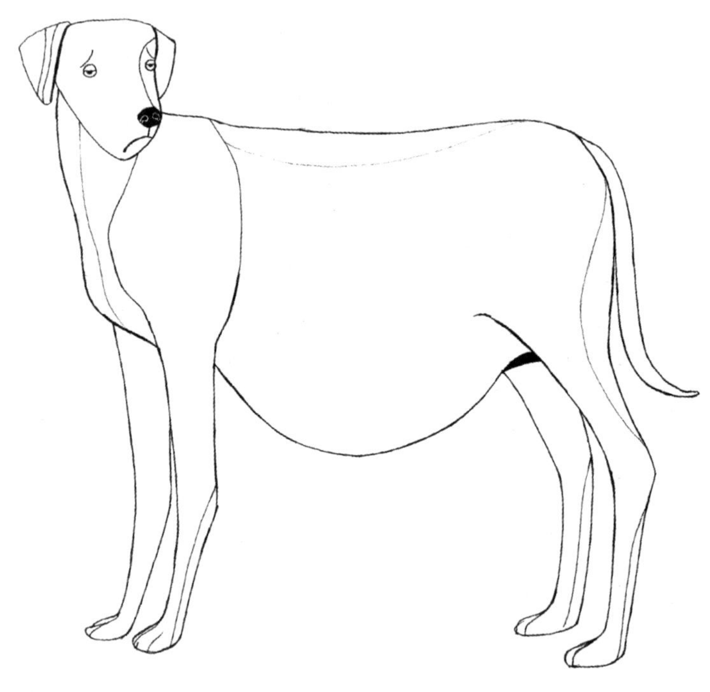

In the next four hours I'm going to have to give birth seven bloody times. Don't expect me to be pleased about it.

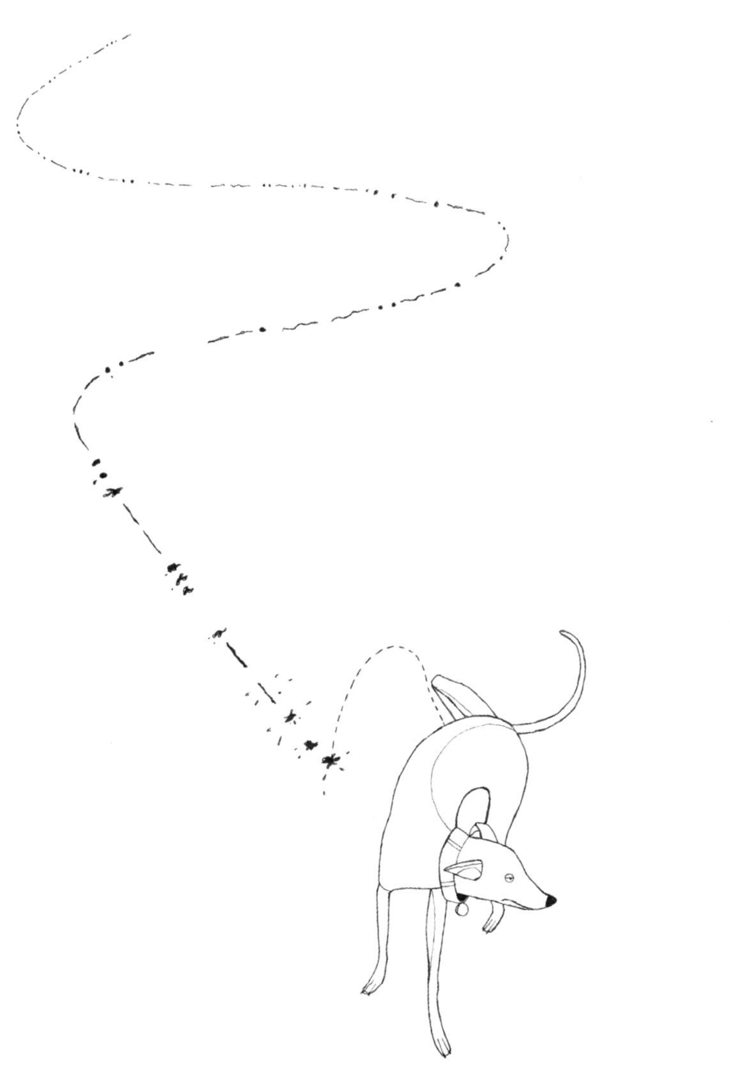

If you'd bothered to learn morse code you'd realise that for the last ten years I've been telling you I think you're a total twat

Hey, cool… a toilet you can swim in

Just because I'm a radical feminist doesn't mean I'm not allowed to look bloody gorgeous

I may be a fucking in-bred moron but at least I beat all the other fucking in-bred morons…

Ooops. This handbag cost 2000 quid
and now it'll forever smell of piss.

If you set the bloody heating at a decent level this wouldn't have been necessary

Must remember… wag then bite, wag then bite

It smells of shit and vomit, what's not to like?

Ha! Found the laxative chocolate. Now the shit'll hit the fan!

If he doesn't stop feeding me this discount crap we'll being taking a detour through some serious dog shit sometime soon.

Yes, of course I ate your car key. And to make things more fun, I'm taking bets on which day you'll get it back.

You clearly have a mild bladder problem –
and I find it strangely mesmerising

I can't help wondering… Am I really a 'good boy', you know, deep down…?

Might as well give me some now, you miserable bitch.
I can keep this up for fucking hours.

Our names? Einstein and Heisenberg.

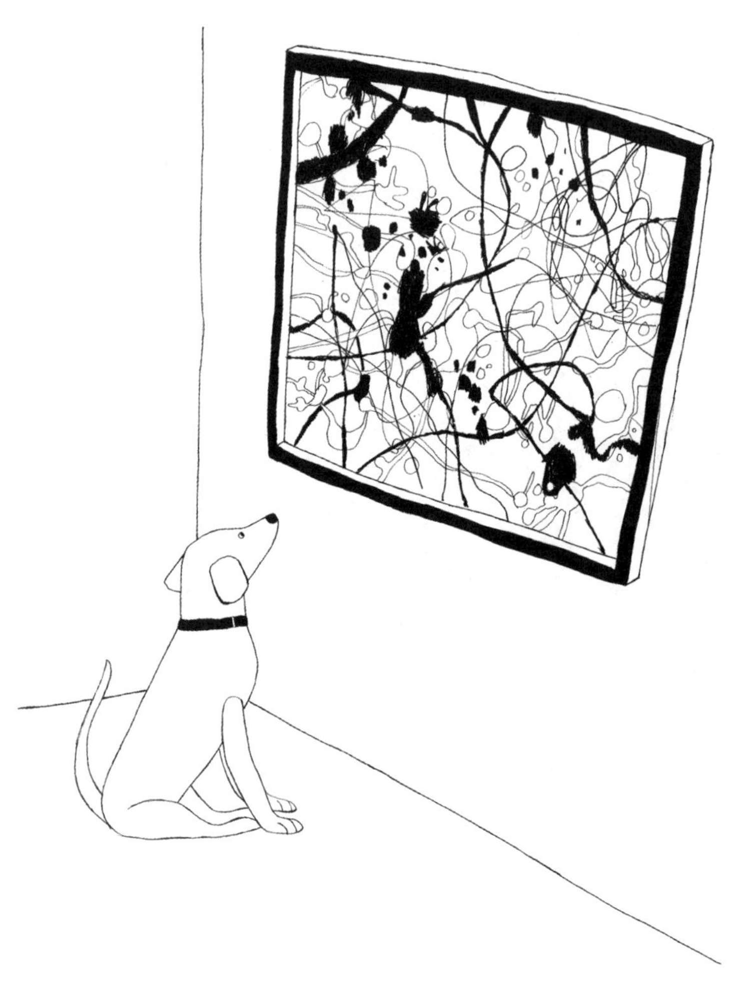

Hell, yeah… I get like that as well when my diet's too rich

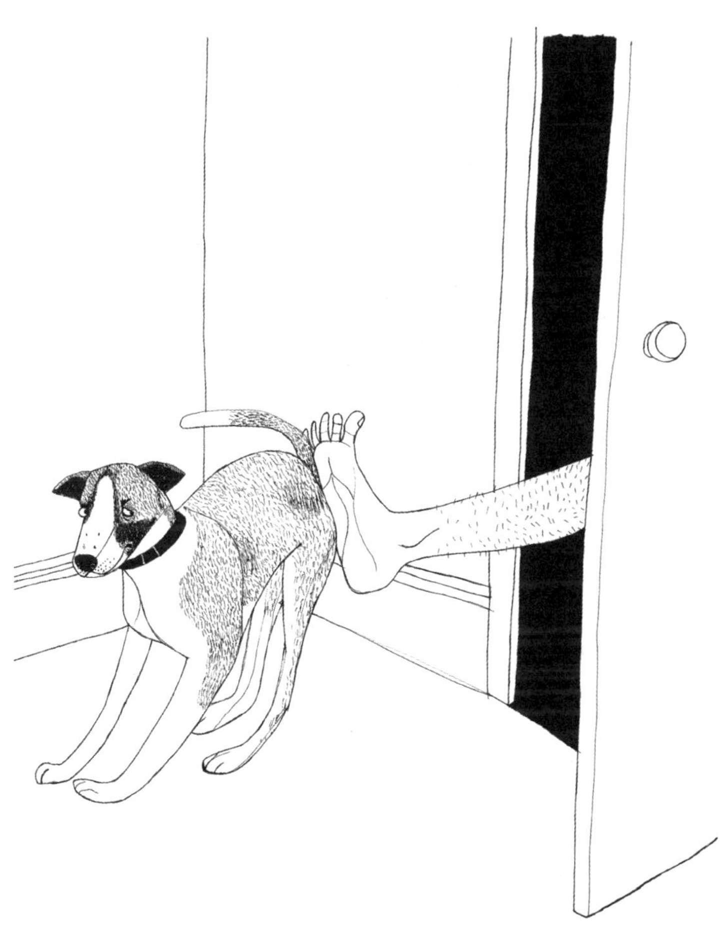

But why can't I watch you two fucking?
You always watch me at it in the park...

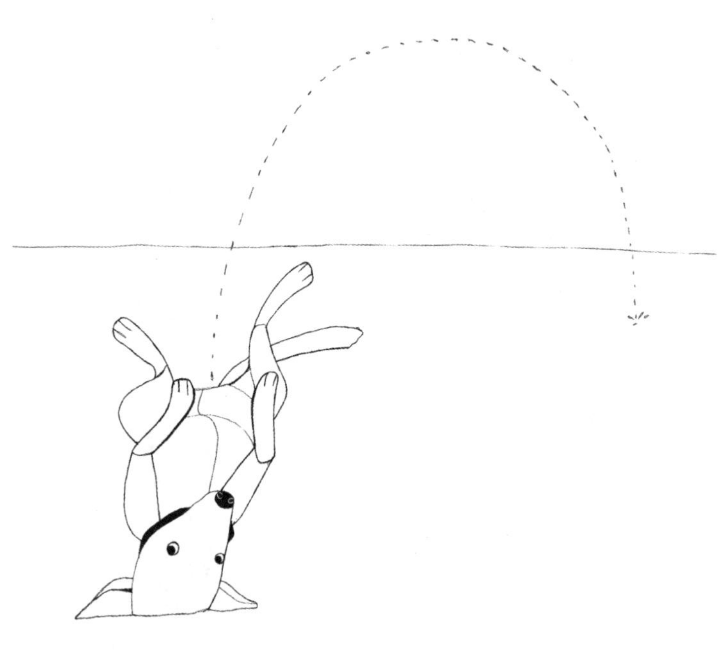

You call it submissive behaviour. I call it naked fear.

It's what he would have wanted

While you're there, would you mind checking my coil is still in position?

I told them they should've bought the bloody taupe

It's nothing to do with bones, I'm digging you a shallow fucking grave

My real name is Zubadiar Al-Muchtadir el Juhinadaar Quahgnal the third, but all these twats could manage was 'Fido'

My analyst told me the first stage of personal development is to accept myself for who I really am

You make me sleep in a cage, crap outside and you put me in the boot of the car… this is my way of saying thank you

Hope you don't mind sharing… and let's face it,
the horse shit I was eating earlier will only add flavour

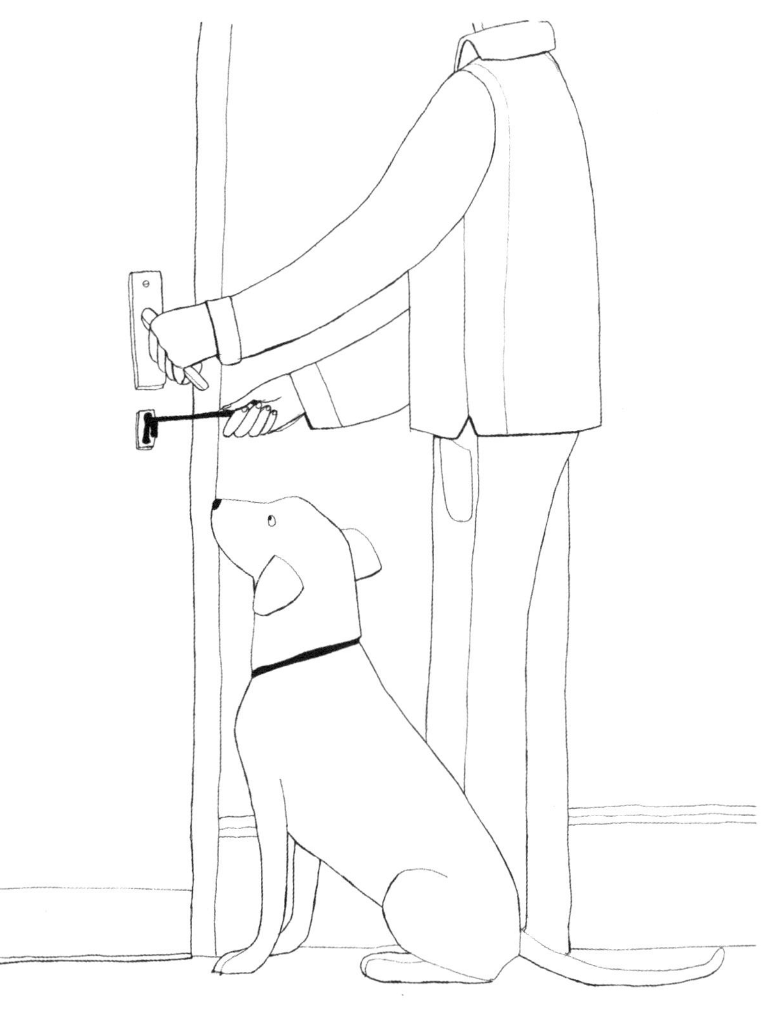

That's it, open the fucking door for me, who's the bitch now?

You leave me out here for fucking hours and then you expect me to be pleased to see you?

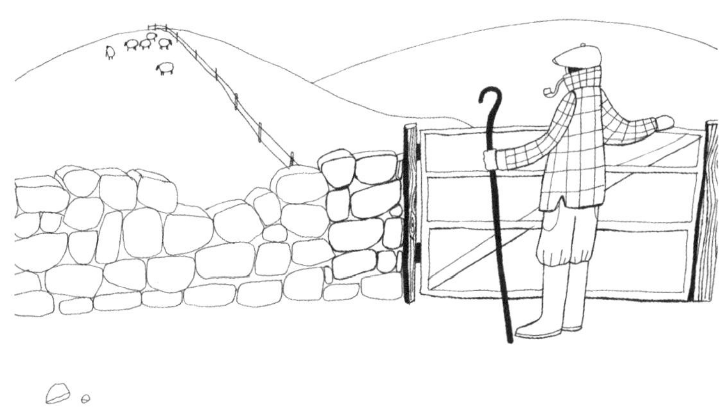

He's my best friend. Who am I to judge when it comes to a man and a sheep?

Not only can I smell that you had a toot four weeks ago, my nose is also telling me you're a complete arsehole

I'm not begging, I've just painted my claws

It's nothing to do with loyalty. The dickhead had my worming tablets in his pocket when they buried him.

It's bad, I know, but I'm seeing a counsellor about my addiction. I got his name from Michael Douglas.

And have you seen my Che Guevara?

Don't forget to buy me some fucking bones… and some of that dog food in the little square tubs… and a new squeaky toy… and… and…

Am I guilty of worrying? Hell, yeah. I tell them they'll end up in Aldi.

If you think the barrel's impressive you should see the size of my bollocks

I used Twitter for a while but somehow endless, incessant barking seemed more worthwhile

Because my mother didn't lick me enough when I was a puppy, I now go looking for love in all the wrong places

Showering every day? But I like it when you smell shitty.

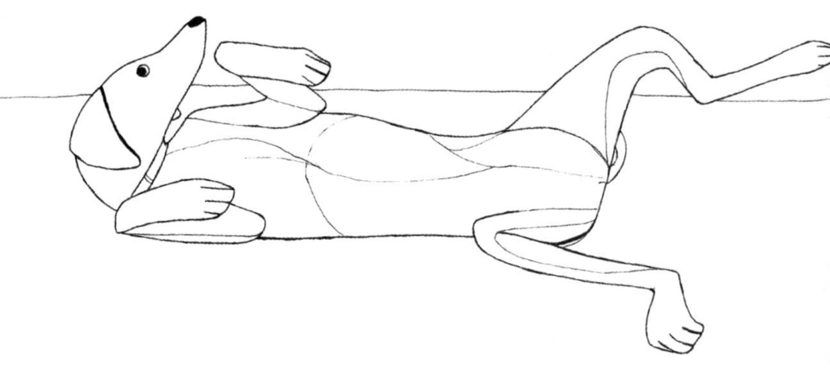

I'm sure they used to be here

Okay boys, first one to catch it gets the clean end

You call it an infestation, I call it sub-letting

I'm not the Andrex puppy, I've just got chronic diarrhoea

Cafe

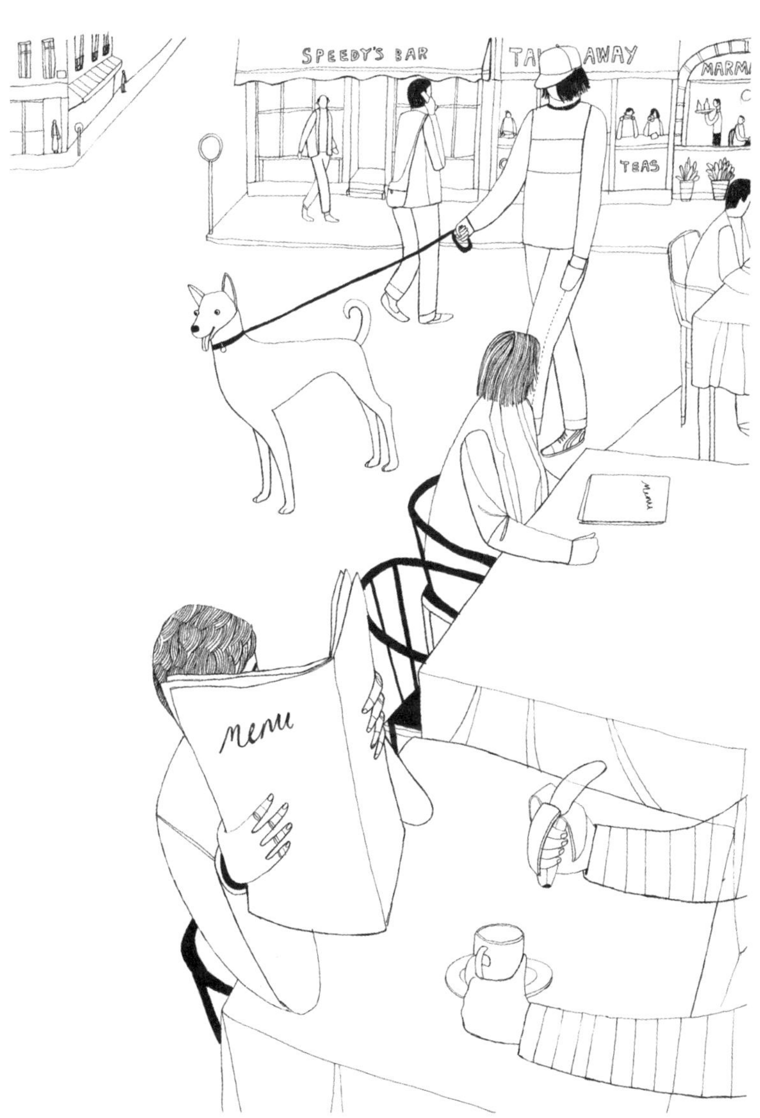

That's the problem with dogs these days. It's all butt sniffing and humping. None of them ever takes the time to discover the REAL me.

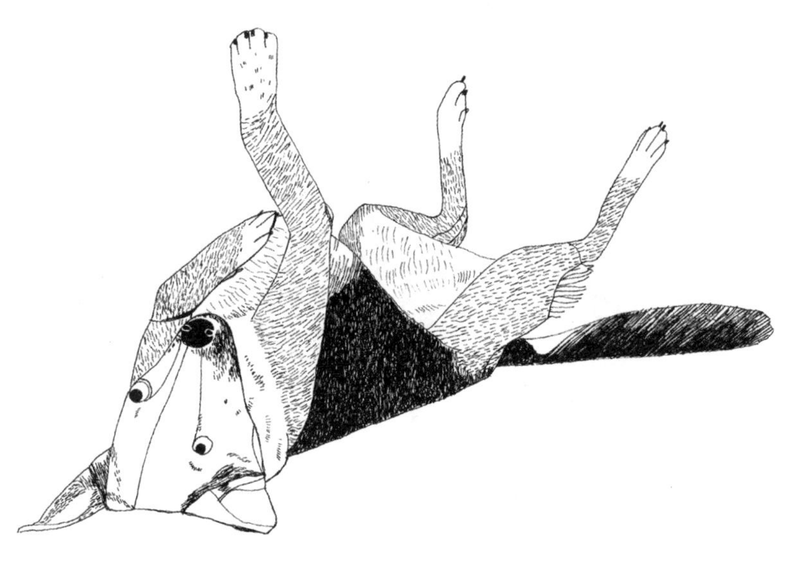

I'm not playing dead, I just licked the skid mark on yesterday's boxer shorts

Face it, you're just fucking jealous

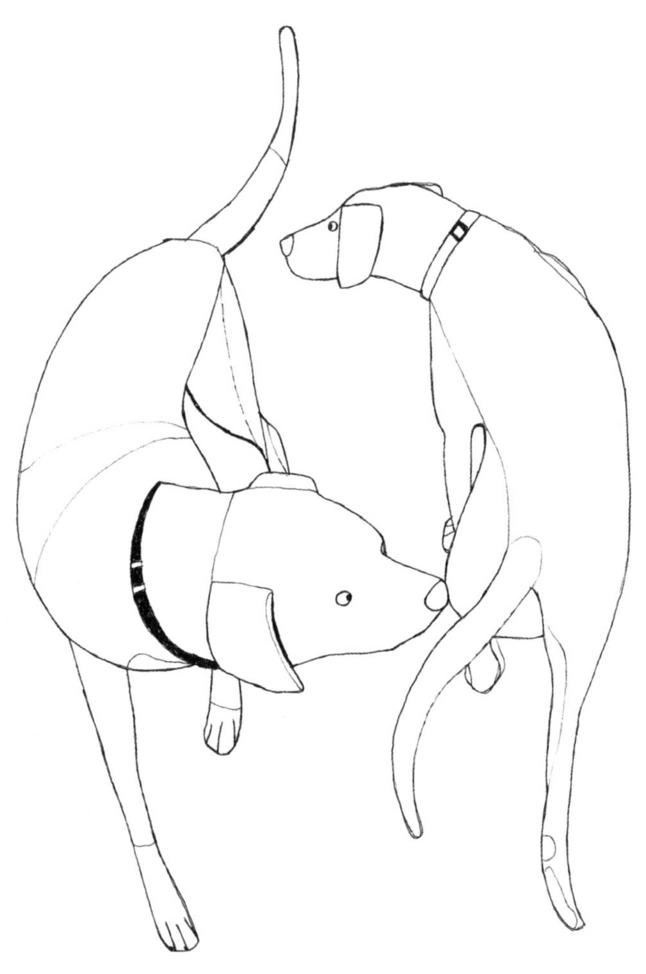

Did I tell you? I once had a trial for Arsenal.